LOOSE THE LAMBS

A Quick Guidebook for Children's Deliverance for Pastors, Parents, Deliverance Workers and Counselors

Written and Developed by

Bishop Dr. Jackie L. Green
And
Pastor Brenda E. Davis

Visit: www.jgmenternational.org

Our Vision

The JGM-Enternational PrayerLife Institute is a non-profit national and international Christian organization dedicated and commissioned to raising up healthy houses of prayer around the world, equipping saints for the work of the ministry, and fulfilling the Great Commission in cooperation with the larger Body of Jesus Christ.

Our Purpose

Transforming and Building Lives, Churches, Cities and Nations through Prayer

Matthew 21:12-14 * Ephesians 4:11-16 * Matthew 28:18-20 * Psalm 2:8

LOOSE THE LAMBS

A Quick Guidebook for Children's Deliverance for Pastors, Parents, Deliverance Workers and Counselors

Written by

Bishop Dr. Jackie L. Green

And Pastor Brenda E. Davis

CONTACT US AT:

420 East Stuart Avenue

Redlands, CA 92374

(909) 793-1074

EMAL: jackiegreenvanguard@yahoo.com

www.jgm-enternational.org

www.raphadeliveranceuniv.org

Table of Contents

Introduction

"And all thy children shall be taught of the Lord; and great shall be the peace of thy children.'
Isaiah 54:13

"...and Jesus rebuked the unclean spirit, and healed the child, and delivered him again to his
father." Luke 9:24b

Oh, how I wish that Isaiah 54:13 was the testimony of all children. Instead, we have a "troubled generation" of children and youth. Many children do not know the Lord Jesus Christ and therefore have not experienced peace in their family, school, community or personal life. There are even more children and youth that are tormented by demonic spirits and crying for help but have no parental spiritual covering to set them free.

I believe that the Church must take on different approach and train parents in a different way to protect the children. Most Christian homes are "hostile environments." Many homes that our children are coming up in are "war zones.' There is no great peace for the children and teens at home. Divorce, separation, violence, hunger, sickness, depression, fighting and trauma have "demonized" our children. To be demonized means that demons somehow have a legal right and entry into the life of a person and can harass that person through various oppressive means. Christians cannot be possessed by demons , but if they live ungodly, demons can oppress and enter certain areas of their lives and operate. We know that many Christian parents need deliverance themselves.

This quick guidebook on ***LOOSE THE LAMBS, a Manual for Children's Deliverance*** is really for Christian parents. Pastor Brenda Davis and myself after presenting a Children's Deliverance Clinic, felt the need to give parents something they could use as a daily prayer guide for spiritual protection of their "Godly seed."

Some parents may feel that casting demons out of children and youth and praying spiritual warfare prayers over their children is too "radical." Well, I say to you, look at the statistics on children today that are being abused, killed, used for satanic sacrifice, and growing up crippled from dysfunctional homes. Better still, take a look at your own children and even your life as a child growing up. Would deliverance have made a difference in your life as a youth? What if your parents knew what we are teaching you today?

In Luke 9:42b, Jesus cast demons out of a boy whose father could do nothing with him. Jesus ministered to children in His day that had been demonized. There are many children and youth that need deliverance prayer.

Let's step up and "Loose the Lambs" so that they can fulfill their purpose and reach their destiny in their generation. EVERYTHING IS NOT A "DEMON," BUT IT'S TIME WE KNEW THE DIFFERENCE! I further challenge you as a pastor, parent to receive your own personal deliverance. There is nothing more pleasing to God than a "FREE HOUSEHOLD!"

I want to say also when this book was first printed by myself and Pastor Brenda Davis, she was alive and had been on our staff for twelve years. She passed in 2011, but we continue to keep her books and teachings alive for many generations. She was an educator and loved youth. She was a parent, preacher and prophet of the Lord. We miss her dearly, but she lives on in this guidebook today.

Praise God, we are taking our children back!

Prayer Vanguard for the Lambs,
Bishop Dr. Jackie L. Green

WHAT IS DELIVERANCE?

Luke 4:18-19 ¹⁸*"The Spirit of the LORD is on me, because he has anointed me to proclaim good news to the poor. He has sent me to proclaim freedom for the prisoners and recovery of sight for the blind, to set the oppressed free, ¹⁹to proclaim the year of the LORD's favor."*

Deliverance is God's method of setting people free by His Power, Word and Blood of Jesus Christ from all forms of bondage caused by satan; which include emotional, mental, physical and spiritual healing, no matter what their age.

Who is responsible for Children's Deliverance?

the Father- Our Heavenly Father took on the responsibility for mankind's deliverance/salvation. God already sent His Son Jesus Christ to pay the price for our deliverance. We must now apply His Word, Blood, Power and righteous living examples to the lives of our children. (John 3:16)

Parents- The father has great spiritual authority over the wife and children. Both parents are responsible to protect their children because they are vulnerable to satanic attacks from the time of conception since they must be totally dependent on others to advocate for them in the natural and in the spirit. God has commissioned parents to be the spiritual protectors for their children and to shape their lives according to the Word of God. Parents are to nurture and introduce their children to salvation through the Lord Jesus Christ. Parents are to love their children unconditionally, pray, fast, discipline, model a Godly example and provide for their children by creating a Christian home environment. Parents are to battle with demonic powers, cast them out, and prevent them from destroying Godly seed and destiny in their children. Even if a child is not old enough to accept Jesus Christ as their Savior, they are sanctified by the believing parents until they come of age. (Proverbs 22:6 & Ephesians 6:4)

Grandparents- Grandparents and ancestors should have laid a strong Christian foundation so future generations won't have to deal with generational curses they passed down. In some cases, parents are not walking in spiritual authority and many grandparents are stepping up and making sure that their "grand seed" know Christ and are brought up in a Christian home. Thank God for Grandparents! (Psalms 78:5-8)

the Church- Pastors and Church leaders should be able to guide parents in ministering deliverance to their children. This requires fasting and prayer, discernment, skill and love. The Church must take responsibility for ministering healing and deliverance to every generation. The Church has been given authority by Jesus Christ to cast out devils and heal the sick!

10 Things

What Should Every Parent Know About Deliverance?

I. **Deliverance** ministry is not new. Jesus ministered deliverance to all ages, and He had a special heart for the children. The LOVE of Christ cast out all fear and torment. We must love God and we must love our children in order forb deliverance to be successful. (Mark 1:33 and Mark 9:14-29)

II. **Deliverance** is not a "quick fix" for child rearing3problems. Deliverance works along with the love, discipline and God's Word. Deliverance ministry is not a shortcut or substitute for Christian parenting, but one of the benefits of salvation in Christ Jesus. (Proverbs 29:15)

III. **Deliverance** can be maintained best in a Christian home. Parents should not expect the school and church to be a substitute for a Godly home. For best ongoing results, deliverance is maintained well in a Godly home. (Joshua 24:15)

IV. **Deliverance** that involves casting out demons or deliverance prayer should not be done without a parent or guardian present and in spiritual agreement. Parents must not interfere with the deliverance workers when a child may be crying or having violent reactions. Parents should be prepared for many types of demonic manifestations that could occur. Deliverance is not meant to harm anyone. (See our Quick Helps to Deliverance Brochure)

V. **Demons** recognize spiritual authority and the level of knowledge one has in the spirit realm. It is always good for both parents to be present and assist in the deliverance process as needed. Demons really recognize the authority the father carries in the spirit realm. If the father is not present, the mother has the next level of powerful authority. If the child is adopted or a foster child, or under another guardian, they too have been spiritual authority. (Ephesians 5:22-32)

VI. **Parents** should give written permission for a child(ren) to receive deliverance. Since deliverance is an ongoing process, deliverance counseling may also be part of the process. All counseling is confidential.

VII. **Parents** should be fasting and praying for their child's ongoing deliverance process. They should also assist with giving the Deliverance Workers any information that will assist in setting the child free. (Mark 9:14-29)

VIII. **Parents** should make sure they are open to personal Deliverance for themselves. When parents have gone through deliverance themselves, they have greater understanding of what the child is experiencing.

IX. **Parents** must repent for any involvement in idolatry, witchcraft, occult practices, incest, fornication, adultery, illegitimacy, bestiality, rejecting the child in the womb or after birth, or other sins in the bloodline. These types of sins can hinder the deliverance of your child. Praying a prayer of renunciation, and turning from any present involvement in those sins, will bring deliverance to you and your children. Our children can be punished for the sins of the fathers to the third and fourth generations. (Deuteronomy 5:9)

X. **Parents** should ask the Holy Spirit to reveal entry points of demons in their lives and in the lives of their children. If demons are there and if they are resistant to being cast out, the Holy Spirit can reveal why the demons have legal entry. Give thanks and praise to God for the Holy Spirit, because no deliverance can be successful without the Holy Spirit leading every deliverance session and exposing and expelling satan. (Luke 4:18-19)

"LOOSE THE LAMBS"

CHILDREN'S DELIVERANCE

(*For Parental Prayer Use Only*)

Demons that Target Children by Age Groups

Common List *Compiled by Apostle Dr. Jackie L. Green & Pastor Brenda E. Davis*

Copyright © September, 20003 by New Generation Christian Fellowship Church, Phoenix, AZ

Womb to 5 Years Old	6-10 Years	11-15 Years	16-19 Years
Rejection in womb	Self Rejection	Low Self esteem/Ugly	Self Hatred
Fear/Trauma	Sibling Rejection	Unforgiveness	Depression/Suicide
Pharmekia (medicines)	Sibling Rivalry	Bitterness/Hate	Cults/Error
Lust/Rape	Me, Myself, I	Fantasy Lust	Premature Death
Spirit of the Bastard	Attention	Masturbation	Mental Illnesses
Brain Damage/Blindness	Demonic Toys	Hate Being a Girl	Addictions
Allergies/Ear Problems	Bully/I Can't	Hate Being a Boy	Debt/Bondage
Respiratory Problems	Quarrelsome/Arguments	Sexual Confusion	Pride/Ego
Eczema/Skin Problems	Fighting/Violence	Achievement	Lesbianism
Deformities	Disrespect	Performance	Homosexuality/AIDS
Ancestral Spirits	Peer Pressure	Isolation/Loneliness	Speed Spirit
Sins of the Father	Sexual Confusion	Fighting/temper/Angry	Immature/Folly
Sins of the Mother	Identity Confusion	Premature Death/Suicide	Faith Confusion
Accidents/Clumsy	Phobias/Fear of Dark	Gangs/False Family	Sex Perversion
Family Curses	Wounded Spirit	Material Lust	Seduction/Jock
Control/poverty	Prejudice	Perversion/Whoredom	False Friends
Shyness	Incest/Fondling	Witchcraft/Occult	Isolation/Alone
Hyperactive	Molestation/Rape	Hypnosis by Music	Dream Thief
Infirmity	Secrets/Pacts	Anti-Christ Spirit	Ungodly Soul ties
Chronic Illnesses	Self-Cursing Vows	Frustration	Covenant Breaker
Medical Bills	Magic/Astrology/Occult	Graphic Movies	Divorce/Failure
Fear of Doctors	Academic Wounding	Cursing/Addictions	I am Invincible
Whining	Stupid/Clown/Dumb	Drugs/Drinking/Sex	Strong Occult Spirits
Thumb Sucking	Learning Disabilities	Demonic Clothing/Fads	Abuse (all kinds)
Stubbornness	Stealing/Dishonesty	Sex-Drug-Music	Female Problems
Selfishness	Terror/Monster Spirits	Identity Crisis	Unwanted Pregnancy
Abandonment	Martial Arts	Vain Imaginations	Eating Disorders
Laziness	Bedwetting/Nervousness	Privacy/Locked Room	Magic/Sorcery
Molestation	Conditional Love	Roller Coaster Emotions	Abortion/STD

Demons that Target Children by Age Groups Continued

Womb to 5 Years Old	6-10 Years	11-15 Years	16-19 Years
Insecurity	Judgmental	Rebellion/Resistance	Little Girl/Boy Spirit
Birth Defects/Retardation	Loner/Unimportant	Worldliness/Macho	Double-Minded
Crossed Eyes	Depression/Manic	Eating Disorders	Body Pierce/Tattoos
Anger/Tantrums	Trying to be Grown	Pornography/Oral Sex	Incarceration/Jail
Irresponsibility	Imaginary Friends	Petting/Heavy Petting	Party Spirit
Magic/Fantasy	Shattered Dreams	Incubus/Succubus Spirits	Self Destruction
Rage/Murder	Poverty/Inferior	Pregnancy/Abortion	Mind Control
Rebellion/Strong Willed	Cursing Spirit	Racism	Carnality/Fleshy
Witchcraft/Torment	Sexual Promiscuity	Sneaky/Lying/Secrets	Runaway
Imaginary Friends	Nightmares	Victim/Complaining	Date Rape
Religious Spirit	Mystery/Occult	Smokeless Tobacco	Time Waster

"LOOSE THE LAMBS"

CHILDREN'S DELIVERANCE

21st Century Demonic Entry Points for this Generation of Children & Youth

Compiled by Apostle Dr. Jackie L. Green & Pastor Brenda E. Davis

1. **Friends and Associations**
   *Be wise about babysitters/childcare agencies
   *Know your children's friends/teachers/sports coaches
   *Clubs (i.e. gangs, teen witches, covens, Gothics and sports)
   *Imaginary friends (spirit guides)

2. **Entertainment and Sports Icons (Idolatry of Stars)**

3. **Television and Movies**
   *Even the PG rating is not always safe for children
   *Explicit sex scenes that seduce them/homosexual and lesbian lifestyles becoming the norm on TV
   *Evil creatures an demonic characters from hell are being introduced to cause our kids to accept evil, even vampires, blood covenants, satanic rituals and fascination with death.

4. **Toys and Games (Video Games)**

5. **Internet (Addiction to Games)**

6. **Clothing and Jewelry**

7. **Dolls and Stuffed Animals**

8. **Abuses (Physical, Verbal, Sexual, Mental)**

9. **Drugs and Alcohol**

10. **Surgeries and Injuries**

11. **Family Turmoil: Violence, Divorce, Poverty**

12. **Death (Grieg)**

13. **Familiar Spirits (Generational Curses)**

14. **The Church**
    *Molestation and seduction, religious abuse, deep hurts

"LOOSE THE LAMBS"

CHILDREN'S DELIVERANCE

HOW TO PRAY AND KEEP CHILDREN FROM BEING DEMONIZED

Biblical List *Compiled by Apostle Dr. Jackie L. Green & Pastor Brenda E. Davis*

Copyright © September, 20003 by New Generation Christian Fellowship Church, Phoenix, AZ

Womb to 5 years Old	6-10 Years
Release the Spirit of the Lord upon them	Release the Spirit of the Lord upon them
Sanctified by Godly parents	Sanctified by Godly parents
Declare they are made in God's image	Lead them to a relationship with Christ
Lead child to Christ	Train them up in the ways of the Lord
Declare they are fearfully and wonderfully made	Take them to the House of God
Provide the best for the child	Read the Bible in the home
Declare they are Godly seed	Have regular family devotions and prayer
Prophesy good over the child	Teach child to pray
Let the child know they are wanted/loved	Protect their minds and little spirit
Protect child spiritually	Protect their eyes and ear gates
Speak physical wholeness	Watch your tongues/cursing, etc.
Break word curses over child	Protect and cover their sexual gate
Speak emotional wholeness	Protect their innocence
Discipline child in love	Provide the best education
Bless the child's generation	Screen those around them
Nurture child in love	Visit their school and participate in activities
Repent of family curses	Get the know of their teachers
Call forth child's gifts	Get to know their teachers
Bless the child publicly before God	Help them select their friends
Agree with God's plan for destiny	Pray for their academic success
Ask God to release angelic protection	Teach them to respect authority
Cancel the devil's plans of destruction	Spank them when they need it/do not abuse them
Declare they are a child of God's destiny	Have family devotion/train the child in worship
Break sins of the mother	Pray as a family
Declare they are a child of dominion	Encourage your child to laugh and play
Break sins of the father	Have family fun and family time
Gifted and Intelligent	Neglect not their gifts and concerns
Discipline in love	Prepare them for the nations
Teach respect for authority	Raise up as royal priesthood
Teach the child to church	Despise not their youth or age

HOW TO PRAY AND KEEP CHILDREN FROM BEING DEMONIZED CONTINUED

Womb to 5 years Old

Declare they will inherit the earth

Declare they will deliver their generation

Child is righteous seed

Shall be taught of the Lord

Break idolatry in the bloodline

Break witchcraft/rebellion in the bloodline

Protect them from ungodly influences

Break sexual sins in the bloodline

6-10 Years

Expect God to use them now

Make room for them in the church now

Speak and pray their purpose on them

Bless the child prophetically

Pray for resources to prepare for the child's future

Encourage their dreams and visions

Teach them to hear God's voice

listen to them

"LOOSE THE LAMBS"

CHILDREN'S DELIVERANCE

HOW TO PRAY AND KEEP CHILDREN FROM BEING DEMONIZED

Biblical List *Compiled by Apostle Dr. Jackie L. Green & Pastor Brenda E. Davis*

Copyright © September, 20003 by New Generation Christian Fellowship Church, Phoenix, AZ

11 to 15 years	16 to 19 years
Lead them to a saving knowledge of Jesus Christ	Lead them to Receive Jesus Christ
Cover them daily in the Blood of Jesus	Cover them daily in the Blood of Christ
Ask for God to release angelic protection	Ask God to release angelic protection
Bind premature death/suicide/depression	Bind premature death/suicide/depression
Pray now for godly mates/relationships	Pray now for godly mates/relationships
Don't curse their fathers before them	Don't curse their father's before them
Don't curse their mothers before them	Don't curse their mothers before them
Repent to them for causing them to stumble	Repent for causing them to stumble
Praise them and encourage them	Praise them and encourage them
Teach them how to receive the Holy Spirit	Be filled with the Holy Spirit
Encourage them to talk to God daily	Expect them to have a prayer life
Train them how to pray	Teach them deeper levels of prayer
Teach them about a lifestyle of fasting	Teach them lifestyle fasting
Lead them into serious Christian discipleship	Continue discipleship with them
Discern the changes in behavior	Discern changes in behavior
Teach them to use their discernment	Teach them to try the spirits
Teach them about the occult	Teach them about the occult
Hold them accountable for their decisions	Provide accountability for them
Cleanse your house and their room of occult objects	Repent of accursed objects
Know their friends	Know their friends
Pray for their friends and associations	Pray for their associations
Attend their school activities	Support school activities
Pray for and know their teachers	Pray for and know their teachers
Encourage privacy but not "locked doors"	Encourage privacy but not secrets
Teach them occult symbols and signs	Tech them occult symbols and signs
Expose them to the power of God	Expose them to the power of God
Break generational curses over them	break generational curses
Confess our faults/be transparent with them	Have a transparent relationship
Pray about peer pressure in their lives	Pray about dating/sexual perversion
Pray for their innocence to be maintained	Pray for virginity/innocence

HOW TO PRAY AND KEEP CHILDREN FROM BEING DEMONIZED CONTINUED

11 to 15 Years	*16 to 19 Years*
Pray against sexual promiscuity/sexual disease	Pray against fornication
Pray against rebellion and defiance	Pray against rebellion and defiance
Pray against the spirit of deception	Pray against the spirit of deception
Pray against the spirit of seduction	Pray against the spirit of seduction
Be open to discuss ANYTHING	Be open to discuss ANYTHING
Develop trust and home of love	Develop a trusting relationship
Teach them to be overcomers	Teach them to finish what they start
Pray for positive role models/mentors	Pray for positive role models/mentors
Take authority over spirit of worldliness	Bind spirit of worldliness/mammon
Release spirit of dominion/wealth	Release spirit of dominion/wealth

20 Ways to Raise A
HOODLUM/CRIMINAL

BY Pastors Anthony and Dr. Jackie Green

IF YOU DON'T TEACH A CHILD THESE THINGS, YOU ARE BIRTHING A CRIMINAL

1. Who God is and teach them God's Word
2. To respect ALL authority
3. To honor their mother and father
4. The value of a human life
5. Manners and how to say "thank you"
6. How to forgive others and say "I'm sorry"
7. How to share and care for others
8. How to wait their turn
9. Never to tell lies
10. Never to steal
11. Unconditional love
12. They must pay for their "actions"
13. The value of work and earning money
14. To take a bath and keep up their appearance
15. They are "special" and have a purpose and destiny in life
16. The difference in right and wrong
17. Healthy boundaries for family living
18. To read and write and get an education
19. How to control their tongue and thoughts
20. The way to eternal life through Jesus Christ

WHAT ARE SOME SIGNS MY CHILD MAY HAVE DEMONIC PROBLEMS?

This list has taken into consideration firstly that your child has had some Christian upbringing, and that your child's symptoms cannot be diagnosed by a doctor, counseling has proven ineffective, your child's behavior has grown progressively worse from their normal behavior, the church has not been able to help your child, no form of discipline is working and your child is out of control. Finally, as a parent you are fearful for the child's well being and the safety of your household.

1. Your child/youth is out of control. You cannot control your child

2. Your child/youth is rebellious and resistant to all you have tried to do.

3. Your child/youth is upsetting the entire household and releasing constant chaos.

4. Your child/youth is self-destructive and self mutilating themselves.

5. Your child/youth is extremely depressed and suicidal.

6. Your child/youth is destructive and abusive with things and people.

7. Your child/youth is fascinated with evil, violence, darkness and danger.

8. Child/youth is unclean, hates to bathe, pungent body odors and keeps room a filthy mess. Demons can dwell in filth and un-cleanliness.

9. Child/youth is comfortable with, drawn to or fascinated with urine and feces.

10. Child/youth hates church, the Bible and anything to do with Jesus Christ

11. Child/youth fascinated with weapons, explosives, guns, knives, fire and matches.

12. Child/youth has become a compulsive stealer and will lie excessively.

13. Child/youth changes appearance and dress, hair, to be totally opposite.

14. Child/youth desires "excessive" body piercing and tattooing.

15. Child/youth preoccupied with wearing only black or dark colors.

16. Child/youth has a change in friends that affect their behavior and decisions negatively.

17. Child/youth curses and is vulgar in thought, action and deeds.

18. Child/youth has become disrespectful to parents and all authority figures.

19. Child/youth has sudden change in study habits and grades decline.

20. Child/youth has begun to daydream, experience excessive boredom or sleep.

21. Child/youth experiencing insomnia or nightmares more regularly.

22. Child/youth afraid of the dark or certain things frighten them more than the norm.

23. Child/youth urinates on themselves or frequent bedwetting (ages 6 through teens).

24. Child/youth is fearful and seeing and talking to imaginary friends or unseen apparitions.

25. Child/youth may have extremely foul breath, snake-like eyes or making growling or animal-like sounds.

26. Child/youth has seizures and bites themselves or foams at the mouth with no logical explanation.

27. Child/youth has shared with you that objects move (poltergeist) without their assistance and that they hear voices.

28. Child/youth is cruel to animals even to the point of endangering or killing an animal.

29. Child/youth is fascinated with drinking of blood and animal sacrifices.

30. Child/youth is preoccupied with their sexuality, masturbation, pornographic movies, magazines and female teens may begin to dress very seductively and very exposed.

Seven D's To Remember
About Children and Youth

By Bishop Dr. Jackie L. Green

1) **Easily deceived**— Because we have not prepared them to discern good and evil and they are tricked easily.

2) **Easily distracted**— We must keep them on target and focused on goals and teach them to make healthy choices.

3) **Easily demonized**— We must teach them about the demonic and the occult so they will not dabble and disobey the Word of God and come under a curse.

4) **Easily designed**—Demonic influence over their physical, mental and future destiny; word curses of failure; or demonic prayers and prophesies spoken over them. A design is a pattern or predicted end. A demonic design must be broken by the Word of God and a destiny of hope must be prophesied in it's place.

5) **Easily discouraged**— There are many forces in the world today and many dysfunctional families and homes that discourage our children and youth.

6) **Easily debased**—They are innocent and the enemy wants their innocence. He entices them to defile and desecrate their bodies, minds and spirits. All it takes is watching one wrong show on television or listening to gangster rap one time.

7) **Easily damaged**— By church hurts and hypocrites in the church. They can be wounded very young and their little spirits are tender and must have spiritual guidance and covering.

Teen Witchcraft in America is at an all time high.

According to www.missionamerica.com:

1. Witchcraft is the fastest growing religion in America today.

2. Our children know Harry Potter, Buffy and Pokeman better than Jesus.

3. Witchcraft is even prevalent in soap operas with occult emphasis.

4. Teens are dabbling in spells, potions, zombies, demonic cartoons/ movies.

5. The Movie "Craft" in I996 featured teen sorcerers and opened a new door for teens to dabble in hard core occult practices.

6. Our youth and children are exploring forbidden subjects in school, on the internet and on the websites.

7. Culture is teaching them there are no rules, no consequences, no life after death, no fear of death, and that they can be a god. There are no sexual rules or boundaries in sexuality and they are taught to rebel against all forms of authority especially parental.

WE MUST MAKE YOUNG DISCIPLES OF JESUS CHRIST.

FOLLOW ME

The First Step to protection our children and teens is to offer them Jesus Christ. Then we must take the time to disciple them to follow Jesus. They must come to know Christ for themselves as they grow in grace and knowledge of Him. **We must not neglect their salvation.**

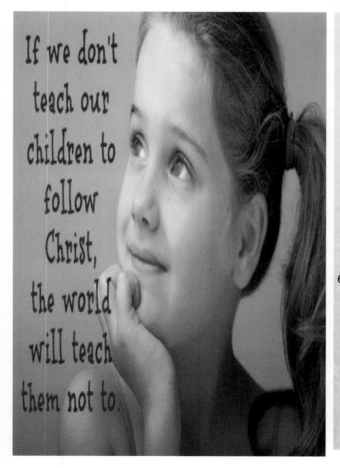

If we don't teach our children to follow Christ, the world will teach them not to.

7 Prayers to Pray for Your Kids:

1. That they would choose to follow Jesus.
2. That they would marry a godly spouse.
3. That their thoughts would be pure.
4. That they would choose friends wisely.
5. That they would have the courage to do what's right
6. That they would learn to manage money well
7. That they would make a difference in this world

Read more at lindseymbell.com

Suggested Reading List

Abanes, Richard, **Harry Potter and the Bible**

Arms, Phil, **Pokémon and Harry Potter: A Fatal Attraction**

Banks, Bill, **Deliverance for Children and Teens**

Barna, George, **Generation Next**, Regal Books, 1995

Benoit, Davis, **Fourteen Things Witches Hope Parents Never Find Out**

Eckhardt, John, **Demon Hit List**, Crusaders Ministries, 1995

Gibson, Noel and Phyl, **Excuse Me, Your Rejection is Showing**,, Sovereign World Press, 1992

Gibson, Noel and Phyl, **Evicting Demonic Intruders**, New Wine Press, 1993

Green, Jackie L., **Church Boy, Church Girl *Bible Study, 10 Things We Owe Every Generation***. JGM-National PrayerLife Institute, 2001

Hammond, Frank and Ida Mae, **A Manual for Children's Deliverance**, Impact Christian Books, 1996

Hammond, Frank and Ida Mae, **Pigs in the Parlor, A Practical Guide to Deliverance**, Impact Christian Books, 1973

Hammond, Frank and Ida Mae, **The Breaking of Curses**

Haystead, Wes, **Teaching Your Child About God**, Regal Books, 1974

Jackson, John Paul, **Buying and Selling the Souls of our Children**, Streams Publications, 2000

Jacobs, Cindy, **Deliver us From Evil: Putting a Stop to the Occult Influences Invading Your Home and Community**, Regal Books, 2001

Kjos, Berit, **Your Child and the New Age**

Layton, Dian, **Soldiers with Little Feet**, Destiny Image

Larson, Bob– **Satanism and the Seduction of America's Youth**, Tom Nelson, Pub.

Morgan, Dr. Patricia, **Battle for the Seed**, Destiny Image

Morgan, Dr. Patricia, **How to Raise Children of Destiny**, Destiny Image Publishers, 1994

Phillips, Phil, **Turmoil in the Toy Box**, Starburst Publishers, 1986.

Wagner, Doris, **How to Cast out Demons: a Guide to the Basics**, Regal Publishers, 1973

Worley, Win., **Children and Deliverance**, Hedgewich Baptist Church, 1983

JGM-ENTERNATIONAL KINGDOM BOOKSTORE

BOOKS SUGGESTED FOR CHILDREN AND YOUTH

Order books at jgmenternational.org and amazon.com

Bullies in the Bible
Tweens and Teens Bible Study
BULLY
Designed by Dr. Jackie L. Green, D. Min.
Published by JGM-Enternational Prayer Life Institute
Redlands, CA

Tricks that Trap God's KIDS
Kids Must Learn to Discern
Book One
Ages 7-10 Years
Written by Bishop Dr. Jackie L. Green
Child's Name _____

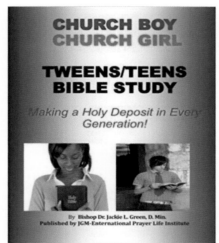

CHURCH BOY CHURCH GIRL
TWEENS/TEENS BIBLE STUDY
Making a Holy Deposit in Every Generation!
By Bishop Dr. Jackie L. Green, D. Min.
Published by JGM-Enternational Prayer Life Institute

WATCH PUPS
K I D S
Pray Hard for the U.S.A.
Prayer Training Manual
(Elementary School Level)
Written and Designed by
Bishop Dr. Jackie L. Green, D. Min.
Published by JGM-Enternational Prayer Life Institute
Watch Pup's Name_____

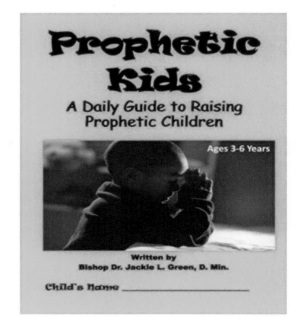

Prophetic Kids
A Daily Guide to Raising Prophetic Children
Ages 3-6 Years
Written by
Bishop Dr. Jackie L. Green, D. Min.
Child's Name _____

About the Authors

In Loving Memory of Pastor Brenda E. Davis

1952-2011

Pastor Brenda E. Davis co-authored this manual and loved every minute of it. She served as Executive Pastor at New Generation Christian Fellowship Church under Bishop Green as part of the church plant team and eldership. She was an educator and high school counselor for over thirty years, mostly in the Glendale School District in Phoenix, AZ.

She loved youth and supported them on many levels.

She was the mother of two adult children, C.R. Davis and Regan Davis.

She will be missed by many children and youth in this generation but she planted seeds in their lives and in their parents too. Glory to God!

Bishop Dr. Jackie L. Green

Bishop Dr. Jackie L. Green is an apostle of prayer and an author of many books and Christian curriculum to equip the saints for the work of the ministry.

She is founder of JGM-Enternational Prayer Life Institute, and Rapha Deliverance University West Coast Chancellor.

She has a heart for the generations of youth and children now and next. She is the wife of Pastor Anthony Green, Second Baptist Church of Redlands and serves as Executive Pastor alongside of him.

She lives in Highland, California with her husband and also has residence in Phoenix, AZ. She is mother of seven sons, seven daughters and seventeen grandchildren.

Printed in Great Britain
by Amazon

39045274R00016